William Thomas Crosweller

Our Visit to Toronto, the Niagara Falls and the United States of America

A Short Account of a Tour

William Thomas Crosweller

Our Visit to Toronto, the Niagara Falls and the United States of America
A Short Account of a Tour

ISBN/EAN: 9783743442733

Manufactured in Europe, USA, Canada, Australia, Japa

Cover: Foto ©Andreas Hilbeck / pixelio.de

Manufactured and distributed by brebook publishing software (www.brebook.com)

William Thomas Crosweller

Our Visit to Toronto, the Niagara Falls and the United States of America

OUR VISIT

TO

TORONTO, THE NIAGARA FALLS

AND THE

UNITED STATES OF AMERICA

BEING A SHORT ACCOUNT OF A TOUR

IN CONNECTION WITH

THE MEETING OF THE BRITISH ASSOCIATION FOR THE
ADVANCEMENT OF SCIENCE, HELD AT TORONTO, CANADA
AUGUST 18 to 25, 1897

BY

W. T. CROSWELLER

―――

PRIVATELY PRINTED.

1898

TO the Friends we left at Home, and found on our return, we venture to dedicate this imperfect little sketch of our pleasant trip across the Atlantic.

W. T. C.

Mid-Atlantic.

W. T. and Annie Crosweller.
1897.

OUR VISIT TO TORONTO, THE NIAGARA FALLS, AND UNITED STATES OF AMERICA.

LEAVING ENGLAND.

THE British Association, of which I am a member, having decided to hold their 1897 meeting in Canada, I thought it would be a grand opportunity to take my wife to see the "New World," or at least so much of it as was possible in the time at my disposal.

I booked our passages on board the R.M.S. *Vancouver*, which was advertised to sail from Liverpool on July 29. We left London on Wednesday, July 28, and arrived in Liverpool the same day. We put our baggage into the cloak-room at the Central Station, and went to see the chief passenger manager of the Dominion Line, at the offices in James Street. We arranged to go on board the R.M.S. *Vancouver* early on Friday morning by tender, so as to miss the rush from the special train from Euston.

Subsequently we called on Mrs. Williams, of Fraser Street, and remained there for the night.

After breakfast next morning we went to the Central Station, got our baggage, and drove to the Prince's Landing Stage, went on board the tender and were taken out to the liner, which was lying in the Mersey. Miss Williams came to see us off, and went with my wife to look a our berths, which were on the bridge deck (state room G).

We entered our names for first table sitting, which means breakfast at eight o'clock in the morning (rather an early hour for us, and caused my dear little wife to be " slick "—a really serious matter considering two hours later would have satisfied her), luncheon about 12.30, and table d'hôte at 5.30. The second table sitting have all their meals an hour later. Supper can be obtained at any time, as there is no special hour for it. A bugle is sounded for every meal, half-an-hour's warning being given. We said "Good-bye" to Miss Williams and started about 4.45 p.m. on our trans-Atlantic voyage.

Nothing very startling happened, but we were fully occupied in watching the shipping in the Mersey, and gradually we began to have that indescribable feeling which I suppose everyone experiences when they first set foot on one of these floating palaces. A tour of the vessel filled us with wonder at the elaborateness with which the gigantic concern was arranged to make a period of comparative confinement one of the most comfortable and enjoyable of one's existence. We retired to our berth about half-past eleven and prepared to sleep the sleep of the just. At first the continual throbbing of the engines was very disquieting, and the strangeness of our surroundings seemed to make sleep impossible, but everything comes to him who waits.

In the morning, about half-past seven, we left our berths and went up on the bridge-deck to have our first chat with the captain. Captain B. O. Jones, R.N.R., proved to be a thorough gentleman, and quite a lady's man, and a conversation with him was sufficient to convince the most nervous of travellers that a voyage on the **R.M.S.** *Vancouver* was practically as safe as the one in the train from London to Liverpool. To his ability as a seaman we had, before we set foot in the New World, ample opportunities of testifying.

The Bishop of Moosonee told us one day, at divine service, that it was entirely through the captain's seamanship and coolness under trying circumstances that some years back the *Vancouver* was taken into the port of Liverpool without the loss of any lives. The agent of the

Dominion Line on that occasion said it was a matter of surprise that any vessel could have withstood such a storm, to the violence of which the wreckage on the shore bore terrible witness. The captain was lashed to the bridge for thirty-six hours, the force of the waves partially demolishing the companion-ladder and chart-house.

The man who seems to be more in demand than any other on the first day out is the saloon steward. The poor man must have been born without a temper. The number of questions he is asked, and the constant tact he has to exercise to persuade people that the captain's table is full, or that such and such a seat is more comfortable than another, are marvellous. If every one wants to sit on the right of the captain, it is very certain that a large number will be disappointed.

A great many people turned green as we were approaching the north-east coast of Ireland (I don't know if it was the effect of the Emerald Isle or what), and appetites seemed, on the whole, to be lost. Both my wife and myself made rather spare meals, as we feared that old bogie—"mal de mer"—might come with his eccentricities and upset our enjoyment. After consideration, I think that sea-sickness is often the outcome of one's fear of it, and with a little determination and care might be avoided, although several of the passengers had rough times.

We arrived at Moville, in Lough Foyle, during the morning, and had to wait for the packet which was bringing the mails from Londonderry. Many of the passengers availed themselves of this opportunity of landing in Ould Oireland; but we had on several occasions visited the island, and did not care to risk the chance of a wetting by going ashore in a surf boat manned by coastmen. In addition to the discomfort of a wetting the chief officer would not say how long he would stand by, so we stayed on board and made ourselves very comfortable. About two o'clock we started again, and all prepared to take the last look at the dear old British Isles. When one sees the land receding from one's vision the feeling of patriotism and love for the dear old country is very strong, and one wonders why it is so?

DIVERSIONS ON SHIPBOARD.

Now begun a series of games and *divertissements*, with which every ocean traveller is acquainted. The surgeon was the moving spirit in everything that was started to break the monotony of the voyage. He really was a fine specimen of a Britisher. Although only a young man, his aptitude for making everyone cheerful, and his general genial kindliness, made him very popular. Filling the position of surgeon on so large a vessel, his constant contact with so many and various characters had given him experience far beyond his years.

For the benefit of my friends who have not been across the herring pond I will describe one or two of the time-killers: Stretching to chalk, deck-quoits, deck-cricket, deck-billiards, and the potato race, all speak for themselves. These reminded us of our youthful days, and all seemed to afford amusement to the lookers on—especially the potato race. The joke of adding a tail to a pig drawn on the deck minus that article was rare fun. Competitors were blindfolded and started from a chalked mark. I am afraid the missing link was found anywhere but in the right place, and when the bandage was removed from the competitor's eyes the look of amazement at the result of his artistic endeavours was quite laughable.

There is a large number of passengers on board, six hundred and sixty-six souls we are told, including forty-five boys and ninety-three girls from Dr. Barnardo's home in London. These latter are all going out to service in Canada. May they make a good start and uphold the traditional character of Britishers. On the first day out from Moville we ran three hundred and one knots.

Sunday.—When we went on deck a very strong head-wind was blowing, and the sea was very rough. The Bishop of Frederickton conducted divine service in the saloon at half-past ten. We sang that good old sailors' hymn, "Eternal Father, strong to save," and never before have I noticed the solemnity of the words as they appealed to me then. The Bishop preached an excellent sermon from Job i. 9, "Doth Job fear God for nought?" A liberal collection was made in aid of the Liverpool Sailors' Orphanage.

There was a beautiful rainbow in the sky about nine o'clock—a sign of rough weather according to some. Although we had experienced strong head winds, we were informed that the ship had made three hundred and nineteen knots for the day. One of those events happened in the afternoon, which always cause tremendous excitement on board. Two ships were seen approaching us from Canada; one proved to be a Beaver Liner, and signalled that she had seen icebergs. The other vessel came broadside across our bows and spoke us. The captain was drunk, and they had lost their latitude.

I got a rug from the deck steward for Mrs. C——, and we sat on deck and had a very interesting chat with Mr. S-m-n, who had been on the Eclipse expedition.

One very popular institution on board that I have hitherto omitted to mention, although it came under my notice somewhat early in the voyage, was a little shrine erected to Bacchus. It was known among the passengers by a much more prosaic name. In fact it was vulgarly called "the canteen." There passengers of all sorts and conditions would meet, and under the genial influence of the "flowing bowl" tongues which were not wont to wag freely became active, and others which were usually pretty hard-worked, were stimulated to further exertions.

PASSENGERS' YARNS.

Many were the tales of more or less plausibility with which travellers regaled each other, much to the amusement of the steward, who was the presiding genius behind the bar. He must have heard some queer stories in his time, and like the ghost of Hamlet's father, could no doubt tales unfold, which if they did not make each particular hair stand up on end, "like quills upon the fretful porcupine," would at least put a dangerous tension upon one's credibility and risible muscles of the face at one and the same time.

I heard a good many of these tales; most of them have gone from my memory, but one yet remains. A passenger who had some pretensions to be a sportsman, was telling us of a remarkably good shot he made whereby he brought down two deer, one with each barrel. We naturally agreed in thinking this a fine performance. But when sporting feats are on the tapis one never knows where they are going to end, and we were hardly surprised when a silent man who had hitherto done little but listen, chipped in with a narrative to cap that of the previous speaker. He had, he said, made a much finer shot; with one bullet he had killed a deer, a salmon, two hares, and a porcupine. Seeing the incredulous smile which went round, he proceeded to explain. It appears that he was firing at a deer standing away on the further bank of a stream. As the bullet passed over the water a salmon jumped into its way and was killed. The missile then sped on and finished the deer. "But how about the porcupine and two hares?" asked the other sportsman. "Why," replied the veracious narrator, triumphantly, "I was knocked over by the recoil of the gun. In falling I spread out my arms and caught a hare in each hand, and sat down upon the porcupine. It was the last time I sat down for weeks." Solemnly lifting their hats the company separated. It was a blow, especially as the hero of the story resembled George Washington about the mouth.

When I say that the canteen was popular, I do not, of course, mean to insinuate that my fellow-passengers were too much given "to looking upon the wine when it is red," as the poet hath it, or that whisky-bibbing was the order of the day. On the contrary, I think we were all remarkably abstemious. In fact I myself, like Warren Hastings, feel *astonished* at my own moderation. No, the canteen was the scene of no bacchanalian orgies; its popularity lay in the genial company one met there, and the opportunities it afforded for a pleasant yarn over an occasional glass of grog, accompanied by some form of the "fragrant weed."

Monday.—Got up this morning feeling as well as possible, and made a good breakfast. Buckwheat and treacle were a great feature on the table. My watch was only two-and-a-quarter hours forward. A sweepstake was arranged on the distance we had covered during the day. Tickets sold for as much as 27s. 6d. each, and the winner of the pool got £7 13s. 3d.—of course I did not find the lucky ticket. There was a particular friend of ours on board—a Yorkshireman, Mr. B——. He seemed surprised when I asked him what a Yorkshireman's coat of arms was. As he had never heard that Yorkshire had a special one, I told him—a flea, a fly, and a flitch of bacon. The first bites his best friend, the second sups out of every man's cup, and the third is no good before it has been hung. The weather was finer and wind a little less cold, but I still found my waterproof very comfortable.

I joined in a game of quoits, which was well contested, and made the time pass quickly.

More and varied games were started, among them being a race. Competitors had to take a ship's biscuit, run a certain distance, thoroughly masticate the biscuit and whistle a tune. You can guess this afforded a splendid amusement for onlookers. I might have been able to do it myself but there was no whisky to help the biscuits down, and nothing to wet the whistle.

Cock-fighting amused us for a time. Two competitors had a stick passed under their legs and their arms passed under the stick, and tied together. They were then set facing each other on the deck and each had to endeavour to upset his opponent with his feet. I think this is very funny when performed on a raft in a swimming bath, as, of course, each time one is upset he gets a ducking as well.

Hearing puzzles and trying to produce an answer also occupied some time.

Several whales were seen spouting in the distance, and altogether the day passed very quickly. Towards night the weather turned very cold, and we were told we might at any moment come across icebergs. According to the log we had run three hundred and thirty-six knots for the day.

Tuesday.—Got up early this morning and walked round looking for icebergs, but finding none, went down and had a good breakfast. It was very cold (I mean the weather, not the breakfast), the temperature of water was forty-nine degrees and air forty-six degrees. I had my matutinal game of quoits, and when we finished we found the steerage passengers were engaged in a capital game of " baiting the bear." Had a chat with the chief officer, who told me the crew totalled up to the number of one hundred and fifty. Quite a little army! Splendid tobacco can be bought on board. What we should pay five shillings a pound for in good old England we get for two. Mr. S———n and Mr. B———y formed a limited liability company (2 shares 1s. 3d. each), and bought a ticket in the mileage sweepstake for 2s. 6d. The number of the ticket was three hundred and thirty-nine, but they disposed of it (the whole stock of the company) for 10s. 6d., and showed a profit of three hundred per cent. The winning number proved to be three hundred and thirty-eight, and of course took the prize (£5). We had by this time become very friendly with our neighbours at meals; and some of the stories told across the table were capital. Mrs. C——— was very much amused with an account (told by Mr. B———) of a cake, sent to an exhibition for competition, getting the first prize and gold medal for concrete.

Sir John S—— delivered a lecture on South Africa, in the main saloon, in the evening, which was well attended. Messrs. S——n, B——y, S——n, and myself were playing whist, but managed to listen at the same time.

ICEBERGS AND FOG.

Wednesday.—I was up this morning and dressed before seven o'clock. Captain Jones told me we had passed a number of icebergs during the night. We saw several, one a beautiful specimen. They were all sorts of shapes and sizes, some like pyramids and church steeples, others with more fantastic shapes. The captain estimated the largest we saw at about one hundred and eighty feet in height, and between two and three miles in circumference.

Owing to the bergs, it was fearfully cold on the windward side of the ship, but the weather was beautiful otherwise. My watch was then three and a half hours fast. We had a change in our amusements. One of the boys from the Muncaster School, at Edinburgh, played the bagpipes, and a procession was formed and marched round the decks. It made a picturesque scene, and a nice break in the everlasting view of sky and sea. Of course, some in the procession introduced the comic element for the amusement of onlookers. Once more we saw the spouting of many whales, but the greatest excitement was caused at dinner-time, when the engines stopped. We had run into a bank of fog off the north shore of Newfoundland. The fog-horn was set going, and we heard the answer ing blowing of passing ships several times. Later on, the captain decided to cast the anchor until the fog lifted. Every member of the crew had his special station, and signal bells fore and aft were going all night, in addition to the fog-horn. An old parson, who was very deaf, passed the time by reading in a very loud voice alarming stories of shipwrecks which had happened off this coast! Such a night as that I have no desire to experience again. The uncomfortable feeling of not knowing how soon we might be run into by icebergs (being then in the main route of detached bergs from the North Pole) was really awful. Even to a landsman unaccustomed to ocean travelling, the look on the captain's face was sufficient index to the anxious thoughts that were passing through his mind.

During the evening Mr. A—— presided at a meeting in the state saloon, at which addresses were delivered by the Hon. Mr. G—— and Mr. M——. Mr. G——, who spoke about Australia, gave us some statistics of the trade of that colony, from which it appeared that seventy thousand tons of sugar would be available for export from Queensland alone in 1898; that two hundred and fifty thousand ounces of gold were exported from Western Australia last year; while about twenty millions of bales of wool are despatched from the colony every year. He told us South Australia was founded and principally inhabited by Nonconformists. Adelaide, he said, was the finest city in Australia, and had the most perfect sanitary system. He related a tale of some gold-seekers who had been prospecting, and were returning in despair from the interior, finding a nugget in a cart rut. It weighed about six hundred ounces, and was worth £2,600. When everything seemed going against them, and they were in the deepest despair, that witch, Fortune, suddenly gave them comparative wealth.

Mr. M——'s address on New Zealand was very interesting. He pronounced it a very beautiful country, and gave a grand description of the geysers. The Maoris, he said, are a very fine race, but idle.

Both of the lecturers told some curious anecdotes about the queer notions the people have of the size of the different

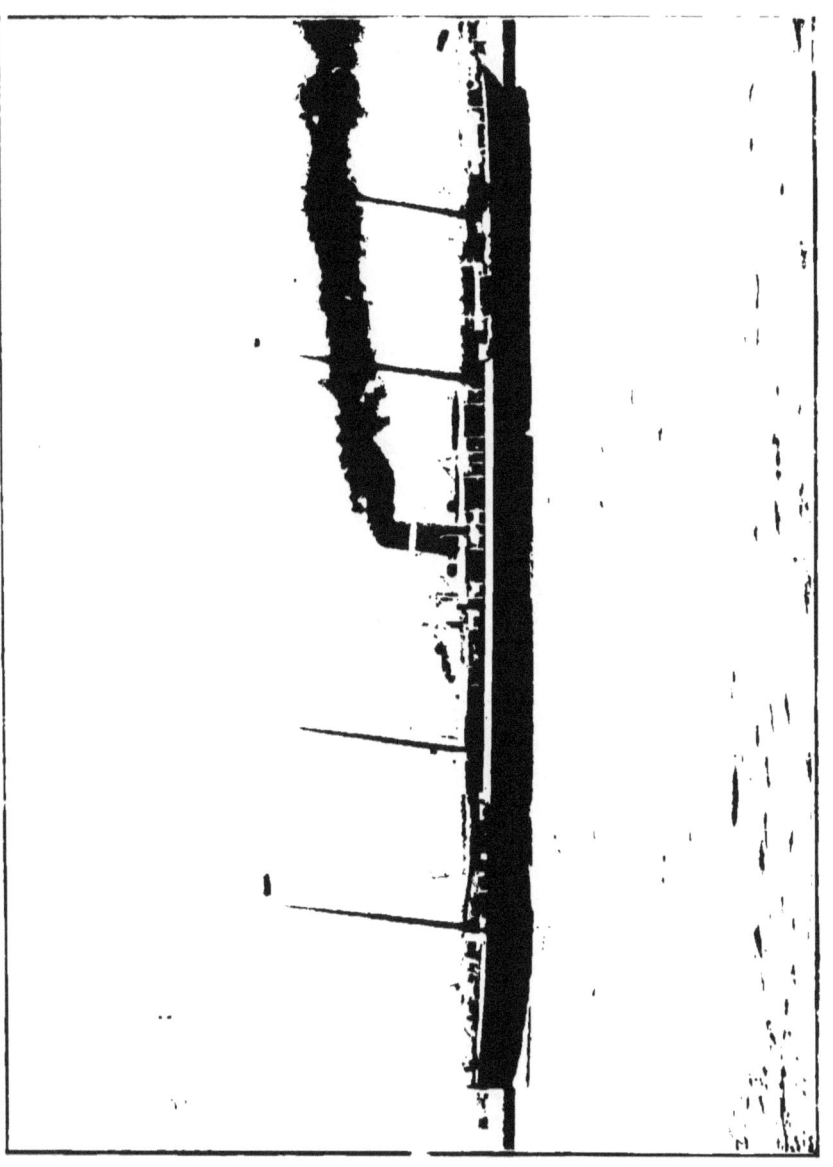

R.M.S. VANCOUVER.

possessions of Her Britannic Majesty. Altogether it was a most entertaining evening.

The fog continued, and we retired to our berths rather early, but I did not feel in a sufficiently calm state of mind to rest. My wife, I really think, did not fully realize the possible chances of a catastrophe, and was delighted that the ocean was calm and the ship comparatively quiet. She was very quickly in her bunk and asleep. It was one of the cases where ignorance is bliss. It commenced to rain soon after, and continued throughout the night. About five o'clock in the morning, I heard a sound which I believe thrilled everyone on board—the heaving of the anchor. We knew by it the fog had lifted.

Thursday.—Nothing of special importance happened this day—the usual round of killing time. In the evening a grand concert took place, which turned out a great success. The programmes were prepared and stereotyped by Mr. P. C—— and Mr. F——, of the *Graphic*, and copies were sold at one shilling each. This realized £6 12s. The original design was raffled for £7 10s. The proceeds were given for the benefit of various nautical institutions. The programme was as follows:

1. Pianoforte overture.
2. Song.
3. Recitation.
4. Duet.
5. Song.
6. Song.
7. Comic Sketch.
8. Sword Dance.
9. Song.
10. Violin Solo.
11. Song.
12. Recitation.
13. Nigger Song.
14. Recitation.

    Rule Britannia.
    God Save the Queen.

The Bishop of Fredericktown presided. The two items which pleased me most were a recitation entitled, "Now, Bairns, cuddle down," and a mirthful sketch by Captain T—— and Captain P——, the latter keeping us laughing from beginning to end. After the concert Mr. S—— and I, with Mr. B—— and Mr. S——, had a game of whist before turning in.

THE MIGHTY ST. LAWRENCE.

Friday.—Up this morning early, and wrote a letter before breakfast. We had been told that the mails would be taken from the liner at Rimouski, in the evening. We had practically completed our ocean voyage and were steaming up the river St. Lawrence, having passed through the Straits of Belle Isle. The river St. Lawrence is very interesting from a historical point of view. It formed the highway by which the missionaries penetrated the interior long before the English settlements were made along the Atlantic coast. On the north bank of the river the scenery was very fine. We began to think that what we had heard about the New World going in for such colossal undertakings was really true. In the St. Lawrence we have more of a sea than a river. One of the Canadian officers who had been over for the Jubilee came to me, and said with pride: " Now, this is just a river, is it not? In comparison with it your Thames in London is merely a ditch." Quite true; for as we were on the north side we could not see the south bank. We even saw whales

OUR VISIT TO TORONTO.

spouting in the river. In the afternoon we attended a lecture in the grand saloon, delivered by Colonel G——, and presided over by Mr. P——. It dealt with the subject of secondary education, and particularly with the students who enter the Normal School for Training in Pedagogy. The great excitement of the evening was a dance on the saloon deck. All the young people, and some of the middle-aged ones, were looking forward to it all day. It took place after dinner; and the dancing to music supplied by the steerage passengers (concertina, accordion, and a piccolo), was very diverting. After supper we remained on deck to see the tender come out from Rimouski to take the mails off. The quarter-master of the *Vancouver* had fired some rockets to announce our arrival; and a searchlight was placed on the lower deck and flashed on the boat as it came alongside. The donkey-engine had been busy hauling up the mail bags from below, as well as the heavy luggage belonging to the passengers who intended going on overland from Rimouski. The transfer of baggage was carried out in a very systematic manner, and was yet another proof of the discipline (almost mechanical) of the crew. We hove to about eleven o'clock, and the tender left us about twenty minutes past twelve. It was a very smart performance, and showed what an amount of work can be done by an organised body of men under proper guidance. After the tender had left us we very quickly got to bed.

QUEBEC AND MONTREAL.

Saturday.—We arrived at Quebec about half-past seven this morning. Quebec is about as far from Rimouski as that place is from the mouth of the St. Lawrence. We had about two hundred tons of cargo to discharge, and as this would take about three and a half hours, we went ashore to have a look at the city. Quebec has a very imposing appearance as you approach it. We saw the " Heights of Abraham " (or as a young gentleman who must have had a very classical education, and who wore a very high collar, miscalled them, " the Arabian Nights"), the scene of the decisive battle of 1759. We also saw the monument which was erected to General Wolfe. The falls of Montmorency (which are two hundred and sixty-five feet high) are about six and a-half miles from Quebec, and are very fine. The river Saguenay flows through a gorge, where the cliffs which form the banks of the river vary from six hundred to fifteen hundred feet high, and create a very striking scene. We began to find the weather much warmer. Although we took a pilot on board we had to anchor in the middle of the St. Lawrence about nine o'clock, as there is only one narrow channel navigable by so large a vessel as the *Vancouver*. It is marked by all sorts of buoys—even branches of trees attached to poles being embedded in the river, making navigation at night impossible.

Sunday.—We were off again at four o'clock, and arrived at Montreal just as twelve o'clock was striking. The distance from Quebec to Montreal by river is one hundred and sixty-eight miles. To get to Montreal we had to go through several canals, as the rapids interfered with our passage up the river. We passed through the Lake of the Thousand Isles and Lake Ontario. The ever-changing scenery quite repaid us for keeping on the boat. We could, of course, have gone on from Quebec by rail (Grand Trunk or Canadian Pacific), but having heard so much about the grandeur of the St. Lawrence we decided to remain. Altogether the time on board was a very happy one From Commander Jones down to every individual member of the crew, all had done their utmost to make the trip enjoyable, and what is more—comfortable. Although we were principally members of the British Association, we could not all claim to be scientists; and as one of the laymen I must say that no first-class hotel could have been better. Considering the restricted resources the cooking was *par excellence*, and the attendance left nothing to be desired. The kindly feeling shown us will be remembered by me, at any rate, whenever I think of this trip.

Quite a large crowd were awaiting our arrival at Montreal. Mr. B—— looked after our baggage and got it through the Customs, but passed the largest boxes on direct by the Canadian Pacific to be checked in bond at Toronto. It was very amusing to see the various trunks and boxes opened, and the contents exposed to view. It was two o'clock before we were able to start for our hotel—the Windsor. This is a magnificent place, containing eight hundred rooms. After lunch I had a smoke, and wrote some letters, until tea-time, which meal we had in Mr. S——'s private room. We started off on a tour of exploration round Montreal, and had a series of very exciting times in electric street tram cars, which rush down inclines at a fearful rate. The fare for the journey round the city was ten cents (5d.). On getting back to our hotel we had dinner and supper combined, which was well served by black waiters. Nearly all the attendants seem to be black. Commander Jones came round in private dress, and we had quite a long smoke and chat. He gave us the following particulars of the *Vancouver*.

She used a hundred tons of coal a day, and sixty tons of fresh water. The daily run of the vessel was:—

From Thursday, July 29th (at Liverpool) to
Friday,	,,	30th	192	Knots.
Saturday,	,,	31st	301	,,
Sunday,	August	1st	319	,,
Monday	,,	2nd	336	,,
Tuesday,	,,	3rd	339	,,
Wednesday,	,,	4th	338	,,
Thursday,	,,	5th	200	,,
Friday,	,,	6th	326	,,
Saturday,	,,	7th	292	,,
Sunday,	,,	8th	157	,,

Montreal.

After the captain left we were not long before we got to bed.

Monday, August 9th.—As soon as breakfast was over this morning **Messrs.** S—— and B—— went out with us and booked their berths for the return journey in the R.M.S. *Labrador*, which starts from here on September 4th. We, Mrs. C―― and I, engaged our berths for our return journey in the R.M.S. *Germanic* (Captain S. R. McK――, of the White Star Line), from New York on September 8th (we intended making a tour through the United States to New York after the meeting at Toronto). We also secured our railway tickets from Montreal to Toronto. It was then time for lunch, as Mr. S―― had arranged with a friend to join us at one p.m. After lunch, while the others were liquoring up, Mr. B―― and I went to see the new Methodist Cathedral. It is a splendid building, holding over two thousand people. The organist showed us its principal features, and, at Mr. B――'s request, played a few chords on the organ.

It was a really grand instrument. After dinner we dawdled about, and toddled off to bed about eleven p.m.

ARRIVAL AT TORONTO.

Tuesday, August 10th. — Left the Windsor this morning at nine a.m. for Toronto, by the Canadian Pacific Railway, via Ottawa. Although we travelled in a Pullman Car, the journey was tedious. Meals were cooked and served in the train. We arrived at Toronto at 6.30 p.m., and, having given our checks for baggage to the hotel porter, we set out for the Queen's. The Queen's is one of the largest hotels in the Dominion of Canada, and while possessing every modern convenience and all the improvements adopted by "swagger" hotels, it has that home-like air about it which makes one comfortable at once. After a fairly good dinner, Mrs. B——'s rice cakes from the old country were brought out, and they were very highly appreciated, Mr. S—— giving an order for some to be supplied to his house in London.

We went out for a little stroll, and our first impressions of Toronto were very pleasant. We met four of our fellow-passengers, and this meeting reminds me that I have not mentioned rather a funny feature of our railway journey. Mr. B——, being the only teetotal member of our party, undertook the charge of the grog to be used in the smoking-cabin on the train from Montreal to Toronto. We made an agreement that no one was to have a drink unless he could produce a certificate signed by Mrs. C——. Mr. B—— was explaining to Mrs. C—— the principal features of the country through which we were passing, but as is usual, I think, when travelling, they both fell asleep—fortunately for his fellow-travellers of the male sex. Of course his pocket was picked in a friendly sort of way, and a bottle of whisky found. It is only right I should say in justice to Mr. B——, that when the bottle was found the cork had not been drawn.

Toronto is situate on a slope rising gently from Lake Ontario, and occupies an area of about fifteen square miles. The streets are unusually wide, and are almost invariably lined with trees. Here the electric street railway is conducted in a most admirable manner. The frequency of cars and the equipment of them make it one of the best in the world. The public buildings compare very favourably with those in other cities. The Parliament Buildings, the Law Courts (known as Osgoode Hall), and the new civic buildings, are amongst the architectural features.

Wednesday, August 11*th.* — After breakfast this morning, Mr. S—— and Mr. B——, who were officials of the British Association meeting, went off to the University to report themselves to the Central Local Committee. Mr. S—— remained, while Mr. B—— went in search of diggings. He found some very comfortable ones near at hand with a Mr. and Mrs. D——, at Henry Street, College Street, which, being within walking distance of the University and other buildings in which the different meetings, receptions, garden parties, at homes, &c., were to be held, were most convenient. In the afternoon we went to Hanlon's Point on Hanlon's Island, and saw a capital baseball match between Toronto and Syracuse. The game was most exciting. We returned in time for a late tea in our new home, and after unpacking our baggage, we went down town with Mr. S——. He had come from the Queen's Hotel to bid us good-bye, as he started next day for Vancouver and the Rockies.

Thursday, August 12*th*.—After breakfast we started out to see Mr. S—— safely in the train. We just caught him leaving his hotel. After tea we went out for a ride round the city in the electric cars. We had a splendid ride from 8 p.m. to 9.45 p.m.—nearly two hours for the sum of 10 cents, or 5d. each.

Friday, August 13*th.*—The landlady lost a cousin yesterday by death, and she is now laid out in her bridal robes. She had only been married two months. They much wanted Mrs. C—— to accompany them to her last reception, which was to be held in the chamber of death.

The heat is still very great, and we have very little inclination for outdoor exercise during the day. Our meals are very curiously prepared, with plenty of fruit, such as peaches, pears, melons, bananas, blackberries, cherries and apples. We have the greatest difficulty in getting our boots cleaned, and when we luckily came across a bootblack (as we call them in the old country), we had to stand in a row and wait our turn. They are possessed of a most independent nature. The charge for polishing boots seemed to us exorbitant, *i.e.*, 10 cents, or 5d., and it seems strange that such a lucrative employment as it appears to us is not more closely followed.

Another peculiar characteristic of the country is that most, if not all, of the washing is done by Chinamen, and having had some shirts washed by them, I can truly say that the manner in which they glaze and get up the linen is simply marvellous. They seem to possess a secret, utterly unknown to the ordinary laundress in England, of placing a beautiful and lasting gloss on shirt fronts and cuffs. After tea we went out for a walk, and among other novelties we saw a white hearse drawn by white horses.

Saturday, August 14*th*.—Walked to the stage and took our first view of Lake Ontario. We soon met Mr. S——, and he told us he had been to the picnic grounds and had seen a number of people bathing. There are numerous watering places on Lake Ontario, which may be reached by railway or steamer, Kew Beach, Balmy Beach, and Long Branch being the principal. We came across many of Dr. Barnardo's boys who were with us on board the R.M.S. *Vancouver*. They were playing football, and seemed to be quite happy and contented. Mr. S——, with that kindly feeling so thoroughly characteristic of the man at all times, gave one little lad 10 cents. He seemed quite grateful. " Now," he said, " I can write two letters home to mother." What a lot of happiness can be given and gained by a little deed of kindness! Bicycle riding is quite as much in vogue here as in London, for on our way home in the car we counted over a hundred and thirty.

Sunday, August 15th. — We had breakfast at nine o'clock this morning, after which we all went to the Methodist Cathedral again. It is a beautiful place, with church parlour, lecture rooms, board rooms, Sunday schools, kitchen, and other rooms attached, and beautifully furnished. Mr. M——, who showed us round after service, told us it cost half-a-million dollars. The preacher was Dr. Briggs (after the service he and Mrs. M—— gave us a hearty invite to call upon them during the week). The singing was fine, and it is the custom here to begin the service by singing the Doxology. During the service a heavy thunderstorm came on, which caused much alarm. One severe gust of wind blew one of the large glazed doors and windows down with a most terrific crash, and as it just followed a very vivid flash of lightning, many members of the congregation thought the place was struck. In the afternoon we had a stroll into the Young Men's Christian Association Rooms and the Roman Catholic Cathedral. The latter is a very fine building, the decoration of the interior being magnificent. There were life-size figures of the Crucifixion and the Virgin Mary, as is usual in Roman Catholic churches. We went for a ride in the tram-cars with Mrs. D—— (our landlady) to the cemetery, and Rose Dale.

We all had supper together. Mrs. D—— told us a very good story about a curate riding tandem, and the objections of his bishop thereto.

Monday, August 16*th*.—Reception Room of the British Association opened this afternoon at two o'clock. It was not well attended, and nothing particular happened. The University of Toronto, whose buildings were placed at the disposal of the British Association, stands in the Queen's Park, and is very conveniently situated, electric cars from all parts of the city running quite close. The reception room was in the main building, with the post, telegraph, and excursion ticket offices. The dining hall of the College was used as a lunch-room. The meetings of the different sections of the Association were held in various halls, each being specially suited to the occasion. The different laboratories were equipped with electric and other lanterns, with the best means of giving graphic illustrations, and where experiments were necessary, all the most convenient appliances were available.

Tuesday, August 17th. — Messrs. S—— and B—— began official work this morning at eight o'clock. As Mrs. C—— and I had nothing particular to do in connexion with the British Association, we took the opportunity of exploring the city. We went down Young Street to the central market of the city, and there saw carriages and vehicles of every denomination and description bringing in the farmers' produce for sale in the market place. The negro or black man was here well represented.

The miscellaneous things brought into this market made it a scene never to be forgotten, consisting of mush melons, apricots, which were sold at from 1s. 3d. to 1s. 6d. per half-bushel basket (the supply being so considerable they could hardly find purchasers at that price), and many other luscious fruits which fetched only nominal prices. The many varied costumes of women-folk could hardly do otherwise than claim the attention of the stranger.

Everyone in Toronto seems to be endowed with a natural politeness— even policemen answer any questions with extreme courtesy. I believe as a typical British Canadian city this has no equal—its clean, well-paved streets, splendid shops, magnificent public buildings, extensive gardens and parks, make it an ideal summer resort. Nearly all the streets are adorned with shade trees.

The directors of the Victorian Era Exposition and Industrial Fair presented us with a season ticket, and also invited us to the opening ceremony and lunch on the 31st.; but, as we had decided to leave for New York on that day, we could not avail ourselves of their kindness.

Wednesday, August 18th.—Went to hear the President's address, with Mr. B—— and Mr. S—— at 8 p.m. Just as we were dressed it began to rain heavily, and I was compelled to send a special messenger to the nearest livery stables for a carriage and pair to convey us from Henry Street to the Massey Hall. This is a splendid building (capable of seating four thousand people) given by Mr. Massey (of reefer and binder fame) to the State. The address was given by Sir John Evans, the President for the year.

Thursday, August 19*th.*—Went in the evening to the Parliamentary Buildings, to the reception given to the members of the Association by their Excellencies the Governor-General of Canada and the Countess of Aberdeen. Had the pleasure of shaking hands with them both, and with Sir John Evans, the President. The scene formed by the pretty dresses of the ladies and gentlemen, the latter with their stars and decorations, supplemented as it was by the military uniforms of the many officers and aide-de-camps present, was very striking.

We met Major H——, one of the Canadian officers who returned with us from the Queen's Jubilee, on board the *Vancouver*, and we left a little after 11 p.m., having spent a very pleasant evening.

Friday, August 20*th.*—We attended Professor Robert Austen's lecture on "Canada's Metals" this evening, and it proved to be most interesting. The experiments were the finest I have ever seen, and great praise was due to Mr. S——, the lecturer's assistant, for their success. There were a furnace and crucible heated by electricity, and the contents of the crucible were reflected upon the screen, so that we could see exactly what was taking place as the various metals melted and amalgamated. It was really fine.

NIAGARA FALLS.

Saturday, August 21*st.*—We went to-day to see the Niagara Falls, the grandest and most magnificent sight we ever saw in our lives. We were up by 5 a.m., and left Toronto at 7 a.m. in the *Chippewa* (a fine steamer belonging to the Niagara Navigation Steamship Company), and after a delightful sail of about two hours on Lake Ontario, we reached the town of Niagara-on-the Lake, at the mouth of the River Niagara, on the Canadian side, just opposite the American fort, the river forming the boundary line between Canada and the United States. After a short stay the boat proceeded up the river to Queenstown, opposite which, on the American side, is the village of Lewiston.

We left the steamer here and entered an observation car (electric), and went along the side of the river for about fourteen miles, up to Chippewa Village, rising nearly four hundred feet in a very short distance. We passed the monument to General Sir Isaac Brock, on Queenstown Heights, and in some places we were travelling absolutely on the brink of the precipices which overlook the river. We got beautiful glimpses of the river Niagara, the Whirlpool, the Rapids, the Falls, and the Upper Rapids. We then came back to the Falls and had lunch at the Dufferin Café. After a short rest we explored the Falls thoroughly; we boarded the *Maid of the Mist*, a little steamer on the river, and went up to within four or five yards of the Falls. We were dressed in waterproof suits. The view was something sublime, and almost awe-inspiring. We then crossed the Suspension Bridge, in front of the Falls, with the Union Jack floating at one end and the Stars and Stripes at the other. Here we stepped upon American soil for the first time. We crossed the Rapids by a little bridge on to Goat Island, and stood so near the Falls that we could touch the water with a stick as it tumbled over. We bought several souvenirs of the squaws (female Indians), and returned to Lewiston, on the American side of the river, by the Great George route (electric cars). We all agreed that we had never seen anything before to equal the sight for grandeur and sublimity. We reached Toronto before nine o'clock in the evening, and it was not long before we toddled off to bed very tired.

Sunday, August 22nd.—Went to the Roman Catholic Cathedral (St. Michael's) in the morning with Mr. S——. In the afternoon Mr. S——, Mr. B—— and ourselves went over to Centre Island, at the invitation of the Royal Canadian Yacht Club, of which, through the courtesy and kindness of the vice-commodore and committee, we had all been made honorary members. We crossed in the Club's pinnace, *Hiawatha*, and had a very good time, tea being served on the terrace in front of the lake. Mr. B—— returned for chapel at 6.13, but the others did not get back till later.

Monday, August 23rd. — President Loudoun gave a garden party this afternoon, which we attended. At night we went to Professor Milne's lecture on "Earthquakes and Volcanoes," which was most interesting from all points of view.

Tuesday, August 24*th.*—Went to a garden party this afternoon, and to the conversazione given by the Local Committee in University College in the evening, the orchestral concert in the quadrangle being very pleasant.

Wednesday, August 25*th.*—This was really the last day of the meeting. At 2.30 p.m. the concluding general meeting was held; but we did not attend it. We had received invitations from Mr. T. G. B—— for an afternoon cruise on his yacht, s.s. *Cleopatra*. We left the esplanade of the Royal Canadian Yacht Club at three o'clock, and spent a very pleasant afternoon, arriving home about six o'clock.

Thursday, August 26*th*.—Rising early we set out fresh and eager to get some general idea of the "Queen City," the capital of Ontario, and the second city of the whole of the Dominion. The streets, we found, are laid out at right angles, after the American plan, and there is an abundance of fine, handsome buildings. We were particularly struck by the completeness of the horse and electric train services. These vehicles traverse the city in nearly every direction. They seem to travel at a rather higher speed than our own trains at home, and cut round the corners at a rate which would raise the ire of the British "bobby," and probably move him to stay their wild career with the strong hand of authority.

But, in Toronto, everyone is, of course, familiar with a rapid tramcar service, and would probably grumble if the speed were decreased. It is stated that the passengers number from eighty thousand to ninety thousand daily. The cars are comfortably fitted, and as the foregoing figures show, are largely used by the population to get from point to point. We made a pretty good round of the streets, and returned to our hotel tired with our tramp.

Friday, August 27th.—We had heard a good deal about St. James's Cathedral, and determined to visit this fine old building to-day. It stands in King Street, and is an excellent but unpretentious specimen of Early English ecclesiastical architecture. There are some fine monuments of departed Canadian worthies, and the stained glass windows are considered very fine. Although not connoisseurs of this particular form of art, our admiration was at least genuine. The spire of the Cathedral is lofty—over three hundred feet in height, I believe, and possesses an elaborate clock, in which the ancient official who showed us round seemed to take particular pride, as though he were its inventor, or owner at the very least. We were told that a fine view could be obtained from the top of the tower, but did not ascend, not wishing to weary ourselves early in the day. Toronto seems to be a somewhat religious city, take it as a whole, and inclined to sabbatarianism. Sunday is very strictly observed. The trains stop running, the very cabs are withdrawn from the streets, shops and saloons are closed, and altogether Sunday in Toronto is as melancholy and suicidal a sort of day as Puritanical principles can make it. The more rational minded among us at home are always complaining of the British Sabbath, but, latterly, the opening of art galleries, museums, and the performance, at certain halls, of classical and so-called "sacred" music, have lent it a tinge of sickly gaiety. The Toronto Sabbath is still as gloomy and forbidding as the English institution in its palmy days.

August 28*th.*—Acting under the advice of more experienced travellers than ourselves, we packed all heavy luggage in view of our approaching departure for the States. We had the trunks crated, and made arrangements for them to be forwarded to Liverpool. This we found a great convenience afterwards, and our thanks are due to the friends who put us up to this "wrinkle."

August 29th.—In strolling round the city to-day a house in John Street was pointed out to us as the residence of Professor Goldwin Smith, the eccentric individual who is always insisting that Canada should desert the Union Jack for the Stars and Stripes. Needless to say, he is not a popular man in Toronto.

In connexion with the earnest desire of Canadians to remain under the British flag, and their dislike to the Yankees, I may mention here an amusing incident, of which I was a witness at a well-known hotel in London, some time ago. Although Canadians, as I have said, are English in their sentiments and loyal to the backbone, it is no use disguising the fact that they talk what is called "the Amurrcan language," and have much of the same peculiar accent which distinguishes Brother Jonathan. Well, a party of Canadians, entering the hotel in question, asked the way to the bar. The astute English waiter instantly replied, "This way to the American bar, sir," to the great disgust of the speaker, who burst out with: "I guess no one said anything about Amurrcan bars. There ain't no Amurrcans here, anyhow." The waiter performed a furtive grin, and I must say I shared his amusement.

August 30*th*.—The day was fully employed in saying good-bye to our numerous friends, buying little presents for home, and taking a last look round the city. Before taking leave of Toronto I must not omit to mention the fine and massive buildings of the Provincial Parliament. They stand at the south end of Queen's Park, and present a very handsome and imposing appearance. In the eyes of a Briton, who is invariably greatly impressed by the cost of things, they gain additional importance on his receiving the information that they represent some million and a half of dollars. The interior is admirably equipped. We were also much interested in the great reservoir at Toronto, which supplies the town with water.

SOME IMPRESSIONS OF CANADA.

Before leaving the great Dominion and extending my tour into the Country which once owned the sway of the Mother Land, but which, as the United States of America, has now become perhaps the most powerful and prosperous Republic the world has ever seen, it may be as well to set down here some of my impressions of Canada, together with some little account of the country from my own point of view, based upon such information of a varied character as I picked up over there during my stay. I am aware that the common or garden globe-trotter, who rushes through a country or views some of it from the decks of a steamer, and then hurries home and bursts forth into print with the most dogmatic assertions concerning its economic condition, its social life, its morals, and the manners and customs of its people generally, now incurs some obloquy. But it is mainly because he poses as an authority. Now I hope to escape being classed with this type of traveller, because, in the first place, I do not pretend to have studied the country minutely, and, therefore, do not speak authoritatively; in the second, because I shall endeavour to avoid being dogmatic, and in the third, because I am not anxious to enlighten the world generally, but merely desire to record my impressions for the benefit of private friends.

Mr. Rudyard Kipling, the well-known Anglo-Indian author, has been recently somewhat severely criticised by Canadians for having christened their country "Our Lady of the Snows." Mr. Kipling may, of course, plead poetical license, but the idea conveyed in the phrase is hardly accurate. Canada is already too much associated in the popular mind at home here with arctic costumes, blizzards, and snow-shoes, and as the crying want of the country is population, it is hardly likely that Canadians will be pleased with any poetical title which tends to confirm the notion of the uninstructed over here that the Dominion climate is terribly rigorous and severe all the year round. Much has been done to dissipate the idea already, and Mr. Kipling himself has made honourable amends for any injury he may have done the country by stating in plain vigorous prose what he really thinks of it. He declares that "it is a great country; a country with a future. There is a fine bracing climate—a climate that puts iron and grit into men's bones, and there are all good things to be got out of the ground if people will work for them." Mr. Kipling goes on to say that what it wants is more men and more money, and asks why Englishmen do not think more of it as a field for English capital and enterprise. Why, indeed? But that, as the gifted Anglo-Indian author himself would say, is another story. What I would say here is that his words seem to express my impressions of Canada exactly. It is indeed a great country and it will be a far greater one, in so far as material prosperity and commercial greatness are concerned, before it is very many years older. Its present population, as far as I could see at any rate, are a fine sturdy upstanding race, the men healthy and well-built, the women beautiful and fair to look upon, as they are indeed in every corner of Her Majesty's dominions. As I heard a colonial statesman say, at a dinner I attended during my trip, in proposing the toast of the ladies: "Woman is Imperial, she rules everywhere. Whether she be found in the streets of Sydney with the temperature at 90 degrees in the shade wearing white drill, in her winter furs in Canada tobogganing or sleighing, or in Central Africa—I don't know what she wears there, but feel sure she wears something—she is always Imperial and charming." I am afraid this is a digression, but I am sure every male reader with an ounce of chivalry in his soul will forgive me, and I am sure no lady will be hard-hearted enough to complain. At any rate, the quotation serves my purpose in so far as it indicates what a Canadian statesman thinks of the fair sex, and the fact that his audience applauded showed they agreed with the speaker. The French Canadians, in particular, with their inherited and traditional politeness to, and respect for, the ladies, will endorse the sentiment as readily as the English born subjects of the Queen.

One thing which struck me very forcibly during my stay in Canada was the absolute loyalty and warm-heartedness towards the Old Country and to all coming therefrom that are characteristic of all Canadians, those of French extraction not excepted. There is no portion of the British dominions in which more enthusiasm is felt and evinced for the home connection and more devotion to the Crown. There is no "cut-the-painter" talk in the great Dominion. All classes of the community unite in rallying round the Union Jack. In years gone by Canadians have shown their loyalty by deeds as well as words, and the little I saw of the general feeling towards the Homeland was sufficient to convince me that they would not be sparing of deeds again, did necessity call. The Dominion maintains a very formidable military force, well trained and equipped, and I feel confident that it would acquit itself well against any foe of the Empire. Although generations are now springing up in Canada who have never seen the Old Country, yet the feeling is that it is still home. It is true that Professor Goldwin Smith has had the audacity to declare for union with the United States! But he is practically alone, and his ideas are discounted. It is not the practice of men of English descent to talk of their affections and their sentiments. They are dreadfully afraid of any approach to priggishness; but, nevertheless, under their Anglo-Saxon reserve it is not difficult to discover in Canadians that very strong under-current of passionate loyalty to throne and flag of which I have been speaking.

As we all know, Canada has recently been making a great stir, politically, in the British Empire, and even abroad. It was entirely through her action that Great Britain was induced to abrogate those commercial treaties with Germany and Belgium which practically forbade us to make preferential tariff arrangements with our own Colonies. Judging from the remarks of several well-informed people with whom I talked on the subject, Canadians generally are delighted with the result of their efforts, and are proud to have led the way in a

G

movement which will probably result in closer commercial union between Great Britain and her Colonies all round, and may eventually bring about that political federation of the Empire to which many ardent English spirits and able English minds look forward so eagerly. It is true that some deny the possibility of such an union; but the fact remains that we are on the eve of a tightening of the commercial bonds between the various component parts of the Empire. And the credit of it all belongs to the Great Dominion and its statesmen, of whom, by the way, it has produced many fit to take rank with England's best.

In addition to what may, perhaps, be called their sterner and more serious qualities, Canadians possess all the lighter attributes of social life in an eminent degree. It has been said that the art of hospitality cannot be acquired —it is a gift. And no race possesses that enviable gift in a greater measure than Canadians. They make charming hosts and hostesses, and have a knack of making a guest feel at home at once. At any rate, all I met had a genial kindness and sympathetic courtesy which went far to dissipate the idea that I was a stranger in a strange land, and to remind me that I was not in a foreign country but among fellow-subjects, citizens of that Greater Britain which has grown up as the result of the colossal expansion of the people of two little islands in the north-west corner of Europe.

MONTREAL.

I have not said very much about Montreal in my diary, so I propose to make amends for this neglect here. It is the commercial metropolis of Canada, and its inhabitants consist of French and English-speaking Canadians in about equal proportions. From many interesting conversations which I had with several of the citizens, I learnt that Montreal has made tremendous strides of late years. Indeed, in the last decade it has been completely transformed. Formerly, as in many colonial towns, fine buildings jostled humble dwellings, and the streets presented a very miscellaneous kind of appearance in consequence. It has now grown into a stately city, and its buildings are of a more homogeneous character. I don't know whether the people are particularly religious, but certain it is that there are a great number of churches in Montreal. I think it was Mark Twain who said that you could not heave a brick in the city without hitting a church window, and allowing, of course, for a little humorous exaggeration—a licence which must apparently be extended to most Yankee writers - the remark is justified by the number of spires and steeples rising in every direction.

It may seem somewhat of an abrupt transition to turn from the churches to the hotels, but after all, while the former minister to our spiritual needs, the latter supply us with creature comforts, none the less necessary; so the change is not so startling as it seems at first sight. Montreal is well provided with hotels, and among them I think I must give the Windsor the palm for general comfort and completeness of equipment. It is a superb building viewed from the outside, but only an intimate acquaintance with the luxury and attention at the command of the traveller within can enable one to appreciate fully the perfection of its appointments.

It is in Montreal that the characteristic winter pastimes of Canada, such as sleighing, tobogganing, skating, and curling are pursued most keenly. I had no opportunity of testing the delights of these pleasures for myself, but I heard a good deal about them from those who had. They were particularly enthusiastic about the tobogganing. The exhilarating rush down hill in the keen dry air sends the blood bounding through the veins, and is one of the finest tonics in the world. The feeble imitations of the real sport which have been seen at places of public entertainments in England give no idea of the sense of enjoyment to be got out of the genuine thing, and even the domestic variation indulged in by a friend of mine who caught the tobogganing fever while on a visit to Canada, viz., sliding down the staircase on a tea-tray, is not so exciting and thrilling as the flying trip down the icy chute, although wifely remonstrances are apt to introduce a spice of danger even into the innocent home amusement referred to.

I should have liked to see the famous winter carnivals, with their ice palaces, masquerade snow-shoe processions by torchlight, and other unique entertainments; but, of course, when I was in Montreal, the trees were out in full leaf, and the upper part of the " mountain," as the culminating point of the gentle slope upon which Montreal stands is called locally, was covered with a mass of foliage. This elevation is about eight hundred feet high, I was told, and houses are to be found quite half-way up.

One thing that struck me while I was in Montreal, and I believe the same is true of the whole of the Dominion, was the absence of any leisured class. Everybody works. Education is very cheap, and even an University training can be had at a price which would astonish British fathers who have to " shell out " regularly for sons who are learning to play cricket and to row—picking up perhaps, incidentally, a smattering of the dead languages—at Oxford and Cambridge. An enterprising man has consequently every chance of making a competence for himself and of eventually acquiring wealth.

The domestic servant problem, which is always fluttering our domestic dovecotes at home here so violently, is also a burning question in Montreal, and indeed throughout Canada. Handmaids or "helps," as they are sometimes called, are in great demand. They are scarce, and the few that are secured from time to time from the Old Country, quickly change their condition and speedily become wives. The Great Dominion indeed is a happy hunting ground for girls in search of a husband or a situation. The mistresses, of course, complain bitterly that they cannot keep a servant, and one lady I spoke to on the subject, seemed quite indignant with the young men who had taken several of her domestics away in rapid succession. I doubt, however, whether the servants in question were inclined to regard their change of condition as a disadvantage. Of course, the knowledge that they can easily secure a berth makes servants somewhat independent, and I was told that sometimes their demeanour towards ladies when applying for a situation, has been such as to suggest that the servant was engaging the mistress and not the mistress the servant.

In concluding these brief, gossipy—and altogether too inadequate—remarks concerning the great Dominion of Canada, which now represents, in the main, Great

Britain's hold upon the New World, I can only say, that I am sorry I could not see more of so interesting a country within the brief limits of my trip. I have been enabled but to give a passing glance at some of the features of Canadian life which interested me, and which, in some cases, came under my own immediate notice; but if I had been able to explore the country and to converse with more of its statesmen and politicians, I should have liked to go more deeply into the subject, and I might have said something about the enormous development which has taken place in steam communication between Canada and other parts of the Empire, and about the various steamship companies whose vessels, of which the good ship *Vancouver* is a type, plying between British and Canadian ports, have done so much to develop the trade and commerce of the Dominion.

Of the railways and canals, I can only make passing mention. The former have grown wonderfully of late years, and have played no unimportant part in the progress of the country. That Canada is rapidly advancing in material wealth and prosperity, the returns from the Post Office and Government Savings Banks sufficiently show. The present condition of affairs is indeed wonderful, when it is considered what a short time has elapsed since Manitoba and the North-West Territories were taken over from the old Hudson Bay Company, which has had such a conspicuous place in the history of Canada for the last two centuries.

The territory then transferred to the Government was almost as large as Europe, and its administration by the Company was so good that the necessary arrangements with the Indians were easily made. Of course, the Company is still the owner of millions of acres of land in the great North-West, and its fur trade in the Far North remains very large.

Of the scenic charms of Canada and of its attractions for the sportsman I had not much opportunity of judging, but I was assured, by those in a position to know, that they are unequalled in any part of the Empire. I can, however, from my own experience, heartily recommend any of my friends who have not yet visited England's great possession north of the United States, to take an early opportunity of becoming acquainted with this, one of the greatest, most interesting, and ancient parts of Her Majesty's dominions beyond the sea.

DEPARTURE FROM CANADA.

Regretfully enough we left Toronto on August 31st, and embarking on board the s.s. *Shipean*, proceeded to refresh the inner man, breakfasting in the neat and cosy saloon of that tight little craft, which landed us at Queenstown after a run of about three hours and a half. At this point we left the water-route and took train to Buffalo, where we arrived, after a delightful run, about one o'clock. With only a short stop for refreshments we proceeded on our journey, and got to Albany about seven o'clock in the evening. Railway travelling in the

United States is comfortable enough. The coaches, in equipment and general construction, are quite different from those used as a rule over here, although travellers in England are familiar with the famous Pullman Cars, and with the corridor trains which are now running on a good many of the great systems in this country. Of course the tremendous journeys that can be accomplished in the States without once leaving the train, the traveller eating, sleeping, moving, and having his being on board, in many cases for a week or more at a stretch, leads the Yankee to despise English lines, and to look with some contempt upon our longest possible journeys.

I recollect talking to an American, in a smoking carriage of the London and

South Western as we were coming up to London from Southampton one day, concerning railways. In the course of his remarks, he expressed some surprise and even alarm at the rapid pace of the train. "Why," I said in astonishment, "surely the trains over your side of the Atlantic go at a much greater speed than this?" "Oh, of course," he replied, "it's all right there. We've plenty of room. But over here, I feel nervous lest the train should run off your darned little island!"

English people sometimes complain that the railway officials in this country are ogres of gruffness, and indeed their abrupt and sometimes uncivil replies are rather trying; but they are courtesy itself in comparison with their American brothers. The guard, as we know him, has some little importance even over here, and is apt to transfix too pertinacious inquirers with a stony official glare, but he melts under the influence of a trifling tip and becomes urbane and obliging. In America, however, he is the "conductor," a person of considerable importance—in his own estimation at least. At any rate, if the unwary traveller should venture to act or speak upon a contrary assumption, his ideas on the subject are likely to be very effectually corrected. Indeed, lack of respect and pert behaviour in menials and others occupying subordinate positions of various kinds are what the despised Britisher has to accustom himself to in Columbia, Happy land!

RAILWAY TRAVELLING IN AMERICA.

Although the long American cars are pleasant for a lengthy journey, they have their disadvantages, and I have heard many people openly express their preference for the ordinary small compartments of the European train, where there is some privacy, although the space is more confined, and one has not the same opportunity of watching or talking to one's fellow-passengers; but then, English people are not companionable on railway journeys as a rule. I have travelled for hours in a compartment containing some five or six people, and, although each has had a good but furtive stare at all the others, yet no one has had the pluck to break the ice and start a conversation with his neighbour. Indeed, it needs a good deal of moral courage to disturb the awful silence, for as likely as not, your friendly overtures may be looked upon with suspicion and frowned down. American railway travellers are somewhat more sociable, and, of course, the French Canadians whom one may see, and the Continentals, who are numerous enough in the States, soon begin to chatter when they are thrown together, sometimes with more animation than dignity.

One very serious objection to American cars is, that there are only two exits for fifty or sixty people, as against six or eight in the English carriages, and the continual opening and shutting of the doors in the former is somewhat irritating. But one gets used to it, and when we remember that the publicity of the American car renders the horrible crimes which are too often committed on English lines practically impossible, it must be admitted that there is a good deal to be said on both sides of the question.

The Yankee porter shares his English confrére's infirmity of incoherency in speech. When you get to a station and hear a roar of unintelligible gabble such as accompanies the arrival of an English train at a platform, it reminds you so keenly of home, sweet home, that you feel inclined to fall upon the neck of the American porter and call him brother. He is not a very sentimental sort of fellow, however, and would sooner have twenty-five cents than all your sympathy.

As in England, smoking cars are provided, and these are generally pretty well crowded. In fact, you have to "hustle around" sometimes, if I may be permitted to use an Americanism, to get a place.

Before leaving the subject of American railways, I cannot help mentioning the "folders" and descriptive pamphlets which most of the companies distribute. They are got up in a very superior style, and have quite a literary air, although sometimes the diction is more florid than chaste. The illustrations, too, are good, and certainly better than anything of the kind I have seen over here.

ARRIVAL IN ALBANY.

After our hard day's travelling we were glad to reach Albany, and retired to rest at Stanwix Hall with a very grateful sense of the comforts which that fine hotel affords. It has recently been re-modelled, and under the energetic and enterprising management of its present proprietors, has become one of the most perfectly managed and liberally appointed establishments of its kind to be found in Albany or anywhere else. About Albany itself I shall say very little, as we had only the one evening to look around us. But it seems to be a fine clean city, with a large number of handsome buildings, as one would expect to find in the capital of the State of New York. Of course, we did not fail to see the Capitol, a tremendous structure built in the French Renaissance style, and having a central tower about three hundred feet high. It is an impressive-looking edifice, and the Senate chamber within is generally admitted to be one of the most sumptuous legislative halls in the world. Naturally the Albany folks are very proud of their Capitol, which, as they point out exultingly, is one of the largest buildings in the United States, and covers an area of three acres. They glory in its size more than anything else. This is characteristic of our American cousins, who seem to pride themselves upon having everything—even their disasters and calamities—upon a large scale. Some scoffers in this effete old monarchy have even ventured to suggest that Yankee humour is exaggerated, or at any rate, based upon exaggeration, but upon this delicate question I will not enter.

DOWN "THE AMERICAN RHINE."

On the following morning (September 1st) we "rose with the lark," to use a popular figure of speech, although I strongly suspect that the melodious songster in question hardly lives up to his reputation for early rising. How he managed to acquire it I can't say, as I believe that many other birds are on the wing before he stirs from his nest. At any rate, I "hae me doots" about him, as the Scotsman said. It was a beautiful morning, the sun lording it in an almost cloudless sky. Our admiration for the beauties of nature, however, did not dull our appetites, and we did full justice to the ample breakfast which mine host of Stanwix Hall put before us. We then made our way to the place of embarkation for our voyage down the Hudson River, or "the American Rhine," as it has been poetically called, although I cannot myself see much resemblance between the two rivers. The Hudson is three or four times as wide as the European waterway, and its scenery is grander and more imposing. The American river, of course, lacks the vines which cover the slopes of the Rhine, but its banks are prettily timbered, and the autumn tints which the foliage was taking on at the time of our passage were beautiful. The United States has been described as a country without a history. At any rate, its history is all very recent, and consequently this noble stream, which rises in the Adirondacks, and flows nearly due south for about 300 miles until it discharges its waters into the Atlantic at New York, has none of those castellated ruins upon its banks which add to the charms of the Rhine, and which have inspired poets, Byron among the number, to celebrate in glowing verse the beauties and historical associations of the latter river. But the Hudson has its poets, among them Wallace Bruce, whose verses on the subject are fairly well known in Europe. The three stanzas which strike me as being the best run as follows:—

' The Highlands and the Palisades
    Mirror their beauty in the tide,
The history of whose forest shades
    A nation reads with conscious pride.

" From Stony Point to Bemis Height,
    From Saratoga to the sea,
We trace the lines, now dark, now bright,
    From seventy-six to eighty-three.

" We celebrate our hundredth year
    With thankful hearts and words of praise,
And learn a lasting lesson here
    Of trust and hope for coming days."

On boarding our steamer, the *Albany*

which started on her trip at 8.30, we were struck by the various types of people who were lounging, sitting, and strolling on her deck. Indeed, it was quite an ethnographical study in a small way. It would, perhaps, be too much to say that there were "all kinds and conditions of men" and women, but there was at least a very good assortment. After the bustle incidental to looking after the luggage had subsided, we settled down to admire the scenery on the river banks and to enjoy the cool and refreshing atmosphere.

I may here remark, *en passant*, that we were in the United States just at that delightful season of the year known there as the "Indian summer," or the few autumn weeks which immediately precede winter. The crisp air was most exhilarating, and as we sat in our deck-chairs we gladly inhaled the ozone, of which there is such a "plentiful lack" in grimy London.

We had not proceeded far on our voyage, when we were enchanted by the beautiful mountain scenery of the Catskills, which are said to derive their title from the Dutch "Katzbergs," which was a name given to the mountains on account of the number of wild cats which at one time infested them. The village of Catskill itself is a pretty little place of under five thousand inhabitants. It had a special interest for our party, as "Sleepy Hollow," the place of Rip Van Winkle's legendary twenty years' slumber, is only a few miles away up in the mountains.

Just beyond Germantown Station we

get a good view of the "Man in the Mountain," a combination of different peaks of the Catskills, which by no very trying effort of the imagination can easily be thought to look like the knee, breast, and face of a recumbent human figure. These resemblances in nature to the human figure, however, are always more or less a matter of fancy, and some of us could not for our lives make anything of the ",Man in the Mountain," while others saw him plainly enough. After a pleasant run through a beautiful country we came to Kingston Point, and thence on to Poughkeepsie, where we admired the fine railway bridge which here spans the Hudson. It is built on the cantilever principle, is 2,260 yards long, and eighty feet above high water.

At Newburgh, some of the passengers

who had done the journey before told us of the old Hasbrouck Mansion, which was Washington's headquarters when he was offered the title of King by the officers of the army; and on reaching West Point, the domed library of the well-known Military Academy—which is a sort of American Sandhurst—was pointed out to us. It seems a fine building, but whether it will ever turn out such fine, smart, and devoted young officers as our own institution at home has done, remains to be seen.

Steaming rapidly ahead, we passed "Anthony's Nose," a lofty peak deriving its name, according to Knickerbocker's humorous account, from the nasal organ of the Dutch trumpeter, Anthony van Corlear, and entered Haverstraw Bay, which is about four miles wide—a beautiful inland sea. The name recalls the curious old verse—

> "West Point and Middletown,
> Konosook and Doodletown,
> Kakiak and Mamapaw,
> Stony Point and Haverstraw"—

a quaint rhyme made with no less quaint names by river captains. Just past Lervington, our attention was directed to the Palisades, a remarkable ridge of rocks in places something like the Giants' Causeway. Their grey stone front rises like a wall for many miles upon the west bank of the river, and forms a very prominent feature in its scenery.

Our steamer made a halt at Yonkers, and when we left that thriving town, where many New Yorkers reside, there was considerable excitement on board among those who had never visited the State before, when it was known that our next stop would be New York itself. We duly arrived there as the shades of evening were falling, and at once proceeded to the St. Dennis Hotel, where we secured comfortable quarters, and were glad of a rest after our long day on the Hudson. It was admitted on all hands that we had enjoyed a magnificent trip upon its broad bosom, and I must say that I should advise all my friends who are going to New York by this route to do as we did, and take the day journey. There are comfortable boats which perform the passage in the night, but it would be a great pity to miss the splendid scenery which abounds on both banks of this picturesque river.

NEW YORK.

We stayed in New York until September 8th, visiting the various places of interest in and around the city. I had the good fortune to meet a friend from the Old Country, an old schoolfellow, who was most kind and attentive. Being located in New York, he was able to give us the benefit of his knowledge, which was of great assistance in our rambles. Now-a-days everything is business—especially pleasure—and we devoted ourselves to the business of sight-seeing with all the energy we could muster, with the thermometer standing at about eighty degrees in the shade—for we found the heat intense in New York. My friend told me that the city is simply like a bakehouse in the middle of the summer.

A story is current to the effect that a certain New Yorker died, and his soul went up to the gates of heaven. He applied for admission to St. Peter, and was told to get on the elevator. "When does it go up?" he anxiously inquired. "It doesn't go up at all," explained the saint, "*it goes down!*" The same night the widow of the departed heard a rustling in the bedroom, and on investigating, found the spirit of her husband helping himself to blankets! The shade explained in a sepulchral voice that he found the nether regions quite draughty after living in New York through the summer. This is only one of a number of tales I heard all bearing upon the same subject.

Another which struck me as being rather fresh, was about a New Yorker whose body was being cremated. After the usual time had elapsed, the doors of the crematorium were opened to see if the corpse had been reduced to ashes. No sooner had the air been admitted than a voice from within indignantly remonstrated, inquiring in vigorous language what the d——l they wanted to let in the chilly air for.

In speaking of New York generally, I need hardly say that it is the largest and wealthiest city of the New World. Every schoolboy knows that, as Macaulay would say, its inhabitants are a polyglot community, and when we speak of Americans as our kinsfolk, it must not be forgotten that, in New York at any rate, more than half its people are foreigners. England and the United States, forgetful of past differences, are just now weeping on each other's necks like long-lost brothers, and it pleases us to talk about blood being thicker than water; but as a matter of fact, the real Anglo-Saxon element is comparatively small. The Chinese in New York alone number over ten thousand, and there are in round figures, 30,000 Italians, while the Irishmen number about 400,000. The city strikes the visitor as being a fine agglomeration of huge piles of offices, banks, and warehouses, these buildings being often of an enormous height. In the fashionable quarters, Fifth Avenue, Madison Avenue, and other thoroughfares, of course, are to be found lighter and more elegant structures, the handsome residences of the wealthy being in some cases remarkable specimens of modern architectural taste.

These select roads are kept free from the marring touch of the tramway and elevated railroad—the trail of which is over all the rest of the city—but are traversed by omnibuses.

We paid a visit to that great "lung" of New York, Central Park, which is one of the most beautiful open spaces of its kind in the world. It covers about 840 acres of ground, so I was told. We saw many elegant equipages, between four and seven, in the "Corso," which almost rivals our own Rotten Row in Hyde Park. We did not run across the typical Yankee of the expectorating kind. I strongly suspect he exists in dramas and novels only, although I suppose he was a reality in the time of Dickens, who, in the course of Martin Chuzzlewit's adventures, has given us some very good character sketches of the vulgar, rough-and-ready sort of American who is now no longer representative of the mass of his countrymen. In the theatres, museums, art galleries, and other places we visited, we found an orderly and well-dressed throng, although, as in the Old Country, art treasures and antiquities of great price seem to get but scant attention, while the music halls and other places of entertainment are crowded.

THE JOURNEY HOME.

We had arranged to leave New York for England by the *Germanic*, an ocean greyhound which yields to hardly any passenger vessel afloat, in point of speed and general comfort. The advertised time for saloon passengers to get aboard

R.M.S. GERMANIC.

was noon, and on the morning of September 8th, we had all our work cut out to get together the innumerable odds and ends which had accumulated during our trip, and which we intended taking home with us. The souvenirs and photographs of various places made up quite a large parcel. After saying good-bye to our numerous friends, we made for the landing-stage, and reached the vessel in good time. On looking round the ship we saw no one we knew, and on reference to the passenger list ascertained that none of the passengers who went out to Canada by the *Vancouver* were on board with us. During the interval which elapsed before we weighed anchor, we were busy making ourselves as comfortable as possible in our commodious state-room.

When we were steaming out of New York harbour, past that magnificent statue of Liberty which dominates the entrance, I could not help thinking of those words of the American National Anthem:—

> "Land of the Noble Free,
>   Thy name I love.
> I love thy rocks and rills,
> Thy woods and templed hills
> My heart with rapture thrills
>   Like that above.
> Let music swell the breeze,
> And ring from all the trees
>   Sweet Freedom's song!"

The return voyage was in many respects similar to the outward passage on the *Vancouver*. There was the same competition for the best seats at the dinner table; the same dismal sufferers from *mal de mer*, one of whom re-echoed

Mark Twain's saying that, if England ruled the waves, he wished she would rule them more evenly; and the same daily amusements. So much, indeed, has been written of the pleasures and trials of a voyage across the Atlantic that little remains to be said. Most of the passengers were strangers to each other, and for the first few days much speculation took place as to who was who—the names of people, destinations, business, and so forth; and it was amusing to hear some of the stories circulated by gossips —individuals to be found on every ship. In a small community, shut up together for a week or more on board ship, a kindly feeling very soon grows up between the passengers, officers, and crew, and on the *Germanic* we were all " Hail fellow, well met," in a very short time;

and when the Atlantic rollers had ceased from troubling the squeamish, it would have been difficult to find a more cheery, healthy, and satisfied ship's company. The skipper, Capt. E. R. McKinstry, is rather a young and good-looking man, with urbane and genial manners; and the way in which he handled the *Germanic* proved him to be possessed of all the seamanlike qualities necessary in the commander of a great liner. Altogether, the last few days on board were some of the happiest of a very enjoyable holiday.

I suppose there is no place like a ship to encourage friendships, and where intimacies have such a mushroom-like growth, everyone soon becomes acquainted with everyone else's peculiarities, business, and social position; and the way in which acquaintanceship between young men and women improves, or perhaps I should say, degenerates, into flirtation, is positively astonishing. Such friendships occasionally ripen into some warmer sentiment; and sometimes, but not often, make partners for life. There is a grand opportunity on shipboard to sentimentalise on a moonlight night on the lounges against the bulwark rails with a pretty companion. Perhaps you may even be tempted to try poetry; but it is risky, especially if the fair lady be of a practical turn of mind, or have a keen sense of humour. No, on the whole, I think it is advisable not to be too romantic even on moonlight nights. This is only one of a long list of things which one should not do on shipboard. Of course, these things are not printed to hang up anywhere. They are unwritten rules, but although they lack type, ink and paper, they are as immovable as the laws of the Medes and Persians, which are popularly supposed to be a synonym for adamantine hardness and immutability. I don't know much about the laws of these people myself, and, therefore, must not be understood to vouch for them in any way. I merely speak from common report. (This in parenthesis.)

Now, there is always a decided disposition to bore the captain with innumerable questions, and generally to overwhelm that unfortunate officer with small talk, until he is on the point of turning upon his persecutors, as even the innocent, unoffending worm is said to do at times, although there is no authentic record of any serious damage resulting to the offender of that innocent creature. Now, this is one of the things you should not do—I mean, talk the captain into a state of fatigue—not offend the worm, although the latter deed is culpable enough, no doubt. The captain has quite enough worry and responsibility on his shoulders without any trouble from passengers. The world is full of bores; and as the community on board ship is a small society cut off from the main body on land, as it were, it is pretty certain to contain a fair proportion of bores, who will insist on telling everybody on board, over and over again, how many times they have crossed the Atlantic; who will entertain nervous old ladies with tales of the horrors and perils of the ocean; who will insist upon singing songs of antediluvian origin at the impromptu concerts on board; who will persist in wordily sympathising with sufferers from seasickness, thereby increasing the misery of those unfortunates ten-fold: who will ask the officers of the ship whether they were ever shipwrecked or drowned; and commit a number of similar nuisances, which are the terror of all on board. We had samples of these on our ship; they were darkly watched, and if one or more had disappeared, and a red stain been found anywhere on deck afterwards, I, for one, would have "kinder suspicioned" their fate. Another objectionable class of people one meets on an ocean steamship are the cure-for-sea-sickness pests. Ships' doctors are sometimes among these, but not often—at any rate, our doctor was not. Some of our passengers had a "go" at nearly everybody's remedy. The result was lamentable. They became temporary wrecks.

There is really no end to the lessons one may learn at sea by simply keeping his (or her) eyes "skinned." When you see an otherwise sane young man bowing to ladies in a particularly ridiculous jerky fashion, and eventually land in the lap of one with an impetus which takes the damsel's breath away, and makes her hanker after a male relation to break the third Commandment for her, you feel that you will never be foolish enough to try and play the gallant to the other sex before you have "got your sea-legs"; and when you see a man holding a crying baby for a lady who has gone on deck, you resolve never to venture upon such desperate undertakings yourself, for the infant is sure to "boss" his temporary caretaker, and wrecks his collar and ruffles his temper. The latter case, however, that of a lady who requests a gentleman to hold her offspring while she goes on deck is, to speak the truth, very rare, for, to their credit be it said, the sex do not care to leave their progeny to the tender mercies of the mere male, whose one idea, should the unfortunate infant cry, seems to be to pat it on the back, "joggle" it violently up and down, until the unhappy babe is on the verge of apoplexy.

By the way, it has often occurred to me—I put forward the idea with all due humility, and apologise to the 11 others—to question whether infants are really appeased by the shaking up which even the maternal instinct seems to regard as an infallible soothing remedy. It is true, the little ones stop their howling when they receive the orthodox "joggle"; but is it not breathlessness produced by the violent motion which hushes them rather than its "soothing" effects? This is not an essay on babies, however, and I must leave the question to be decided elsewhere. But before I leave the subject, I must say that the baby on board ship is really an unmitigated nuisance. It is true, of course, that we all started life as babies. We read in some journals which give biographies of celebrated men, that they started life with a half-crown in their pockets. They must be exceptions to the general rule, I suppose, since most of us begin our earthly career without any pockets at all, and take our first look at the world from the vacant rolling eyes of the common, fat, red, snub-nosed infant. Therefore, we ought to have sympathy with that irrepressible little creature. But, nevertheless, when he or she cries all night in the cabin of a ship—ships' cabins have thin partitions, recollect—we momentarily forget the love we ought to bear the vociferous babe, and consign him to Davy Jones—a gentleman, I believe, of uncertain antecedents, who is supposed to reside at the bottom of the ocean somewhere.

Talking of the thinness of the cabin partitions, I may say they are substantial enough in their way, but, considered as walls, they are weak. If walls have ears, cabin partitions have more. As you lie in your bunk you should be careful how you talk, especially about your neighbour, who may chance to hear, which is unpleasant, as you may not always be dwelling upon the bright side of his character, and saying what a nice, kind, agreeable fellow he is.

One of the passengers confided to me an amusing incident, which proves how wary one ought to be in this respect. It seems he had stayed up pretty late one night with a companion in the smoking-room, playing cards, and taking aboard whiskeys and sodas, until the latter was somewhat exhilarated, and in retiring steered a rather eccentric course to his cabin. In the morning, my acquaintance was telling his son, who had retired early, of the previous night's proceedings, and was not a little satirical in describing the demeanour of his companion, who had imbibed too freely. In the midst of the narrative he was thunderstruck to hear a smothered exclamation of indignation come from the other side of the cabin partition. He did not know that the man whom he was talking about was berthed "next door"! At the time I was told the story, the two were strangers who never spoke as they passed by. Whether they have since "made it up," I know not; but the incident "makes you careful, doesn't it," as the old comic song saith, and teacheth that the unruly member should be bridled on board ship in particular.

One personality which is extremely disagreeable within the limited area of a ship is the meddlesome man, who attempts to teach the officers navigation, and would, no doubt, on shore spend hours in instructing an elderly hen how to lay eggs. He is sometimes disposed to show you how the ship may be made to lay two—ahem! I beg pardon—lay to. He sometimes causes trouble, and is occasionally put to confusion himself.

I was once on board a vessel which was slowly forging ahead into Southampton docks. Near me was a typical meddlesome man, and he was engaged in meddling with a mysterious little lever which projected inwards over the rail of the ship near the bow. He was playing with the polished handle while talking to a friend, and speculating as to its uses. Suddenly there was a shout and a splash. The passengers rushed to the side of the vessel and beheld in the water a life-buoy, with a little mast and a red flag attached. It was the "man overboard" buoy which had been dropped into the water. No one was more astonished than the culprit at the consequence of his action, and, to do him justice, I must say he had the saving grace to look somewhat embarrassed. The buoy was rescued with some trouble, and I venture to think that this particular "meddlesome man" was partially cured of his failing.

These few reflections and recollections I have set down as they occurred to me, without any particular regard to the order in which they come, but I trust the friends who honour me by perusing these humble pages will pardon all shortcomings. Some people make a journal of their doings on shipboard with the idea that, on reaching London or any other great city to which they may be bound, they have only to announce the fact that they have such a document, to be besieged by publishers eager to give it to an expectant world. I have never cherished such a delusion, so I have not been disappointed. I have been able to pursue the even tenor of my way since I arrived in England without absolutely tumbling over frantic publishers. They have not molested me in any way, and now that these lines are in print, I feel that I am safe from any such troubles.

Having been brought up in good old substantial England, the preparation which we had in Toronto (which combines the substantiality of Great Britain with the go-aheadness of the States) was really necessary for our proper appreciation of New York with all its bustle. When we arrived in England and set foot upon our native soil, our joy at returning to the Old Country was mingled with some passing regrets that we had come to the end of so delightful a holiday, which had made us acquainted with some portion of Greater Britain, and in some measure with that great nation which, while it no longer owns the sway of our Queen, yet speaks the same language as ourselves, and inherits the same ideas and traditions.

But here we are once more at dear old Sidcup, and here we will say good-bye, trusting that these few discursive notes, with all their faults, will have given my readers some little idea of the happy time my wife and I spent on our first visit to the New World—that land of infinite possibilities.

FINIS.

www.ingramcontent.com/pod-product-compliance
Lightning Source LLC
Chambersburg PA
CBHW020830190426
43197CB00037B/1231